EARLY AMERICAN MELODIES FOR FLUTE AND GUITAR

MB21322

BY LEO WELCH

Visit us on the Web at www.melbay.com or www.billsmusicshelf.com

Table of Contents

Edward Riley's Flute Melodies

Music making in the United States in the early part of the 19th-century was strongly influenced by European sources. Immigrant composers/publishers, such as flutist Edward Riley (1769-1829) from London, settled in New York and developed a publishing house that produced countless songs, tunes from operas, arrangements and instrumental works. This music was performed at various social occasions including weddings, dances and newly organized concert series. Included in this number of published works are four volumes of flute melodies entitled *Riley's Flute Melodies*. The arrangements in this edition are drawn from volumes one and two, which were published from 1816 to 1817.

Riley's Flute Melodies consists of collections of popular melodies from that era, airs and dances. The book was probably used as jazz musicians use lead sheets to develop spontaneous arrangements of pieces depending upon the occasion, and musicians at hand. Judging from the examination of many scores from this era, flutists and guitarists in early America certainly performed together. Typically, the flutist would play melodies while the guitarists would provide simple accompaniment patterns. Depending upon the skill of the guitarist, accompaniments would possibly be improvised or arranged according to the conventions of the time. Fortunately, there is a contemporary European model for guitar arrangement in Fernando Sor's *Method for the Spanish Guitar*.

Sor's *Method* provides detailed instructions to the guitarist on both arranging pre-existing music for guitar as well as creating new arrangements. Specific instructions are provided for creating special textures and unique accompaniments possible only on the guitar. Thus, all of the music in this Mel Bay publication is arranged as a well-trained guitarist from this era may have arranged it with the techniques, harmonic and compositional practices in use during this time.

In keeping with performance practices of traditional music, these arrangements are organized into sets of pieces as they may have been performed during this era. According to these conventions, the mood and character of the pieces are considered to be more important than the key relationships between the pieces. The *Melodies from the Continent* are all works influenced by the music of France. The *Jigs, Slow Airs,* and *March* sets are comprised of popular dances and tunes from the era. In keeping with the spirit of freedom in this early form of American music, the guitarist and flutist are invited to create their own unique pairings of melodies from these arrangements.

Sources
Dichter, Harry and Elliott Shapiro. *Handbook of Early American Sheet Music 1768-1889*. New York: Dover Publications, 1977.

Wolf, Richard J. *Secular Music in America 1801-1825: A Bibliography*. New York: The New York Public Library. Astor, Lenox and Tilden Foundations, 1964.

Sor, Ferdinand. *Method for the Spanish Guitar*. Translated by A. Merrick. London: Richard Cocks and Co., 1832 and 1850; reprint, New York: Da Capo Press, 1971.

Acknowledgments
The author thanks flutist Wendell Dobbs who first brought these delightful miniatures to his attention. Thanks as well go to Wendell for his efforts in editing this manuscript.

Leo Welch

Leo Welch, guitarist, is in demand as a composer/arranger, educator and performer throughout the United States. As an editor and arranger, Dr. Welch has published over 35 arrangements and editions of solo, chamber, and guitar ensemble works with the FJH Music Company, Mel Bay Publications, Tuscany Publications (Theodore Presser), and Class Guitar Resources. Welch's arrangement of G.P. Telemann's *Trio Sonata in A Minor* was featured in a guitar chamber music concert at the White House in December of 2004. As an educator and pedagogue, he has presented sessions at many regional and national MENC conferences concerning teaching class guitar in the public schools. He has also written articles relating to guitar education and guitar pedagogy that have been featured in the *American String Teacher, Soundboard* (Guitar Foundation of America), and *GuitArt International* periodicals. Welch remains active as a performer with concert appearances and lecture performances throughout the United States at guitar festivals and universities. Welch currently serves as assistant dean at the Florida State University College of Music. In addition to his administrative duties, Welch also teaches music theory and guitar ensemble.

Melodies From the Continent

L'été

Riley
arr. Leo Welch

La Virginella

Riley
arr. Leo Welch

La Cythère

Riley
arr. Leo Welch

Jigs

Bucks of Westmeath

Riley
arr. Leo Welch

The President's Welcome to York

Riley
arr. Leo Welch

15

The Priest In His Boots

Riley
arr. Leo Welch

Slow Airs

She Rose and Loote Me In

Riley
arr. Leo Welch

Fl.
Gtr.
C III
C I
cresc. accel.
tr

The 14th of October

Riley
arr. Leo Welch

Fl.
Gtr.
20
XII
2
3
mf
25
Fl.
Gtr.
p
1 2 4
3
2 4
30
Fl.
Gtr.
cresc.
0
0
CIII
1 1
0
cresc.

Marches

March in Forty Thieves

This page has been left blank to
avoid an awkward page turn.

White Cockade

Fl.
Gtr.
20
mp
25
Fl.
Gtr.
p
30
Fl.
Gtr.
CII

Bonny Charle

Fl.
Gtr.
last strain also used as intro figure
31
40
48
54
58

Bill's Music Shelf • www.BILLSMUSICSHELF.com

Bill's Music Shelf • www.BILLSMUSICSHELF.com

BILL'S
MUSIC
SHELF
UNIQUELY INTERESTING MUSIC!

Made in the USA
Monee, IL
07 July 2026

56551279R00020